The Hedgehog Rescuers
Published in 2025 by
Tiny Tree Books
West Wing Studios
Unit 166, The Mall
Luton, LU1 2TL
tinytreebooks.com

The HEDGEHOG RESCUERS!

Written by Sarah Oliver
for Lily, Ollie, Mia, Dottie and Demi

Illustrated by Juliet Prentice
for Seb and Miri

TINY TREE

Joe and his brother Max were painting robots
when Joe spotted something interesting.

"HEDGEHOG RESCUERS NEEDED.
Could you set up a hedgehog sanctuary to help
sick and injured hedgehogs?"

"YES!"

replied Max.

They found lots of books about hedgehogs and how to look after them.

"We can build some hedgehog houses; to start with we just need some large plastic boxes with holes in them, plastic sheeting and some straw," said Joe. "Then we can make some wooden ones."

"It says to put a twig by the doorway. If it moves, then you know that a hedgehog has moved in," said Max. "That's a good tip."

"I'll stop using chemicals in the garden such as slug pellets, because they're poisonous to hedgehogs," added Mum.

IDENTIFICATION

WILDLIFE

EDGEHOGS

STOP!

hedgeho[g]
rescu[e]

"Don't cut all of the grass!" said Joe. "We need an area with long grass and wildflowers for grasshoppers and caterpillars. They'll be the hedgehogs' food.

"We should build a log pile in the corner," said Max. "Somewhere for them to hibernate and have babies."

log pile

leaf pile

home

pond

pen

wild grass

bug hotel

"I'll cut a few holes at the bottom of the fences," said Mum, "so they can go into different gardens."

"I've sent a leaflet to our neighbours because
we need to become a hedgehog network,"
said Joe. "We need to all work together to help
the hedgehogs and make sure there's no litter or
netting in which they could get caught."

"They can travel for a mile every night," said Max.
"That would make me so tired!"

"I'm digging a pond, with sloping sides and ramps so the hedgehogs can climb out," said Max. "Hedgehogs are really good swimmers and they'll like drinking the water too."

"I'm going to make a tower of leaves next to the compost heap; the hedgehogs will love it," said Joe.

"This bug hotel is going to have loads of mini beasts. It'll have worms, beetles, spiders and woodlice for the hedgehogs to eat," said Joe.

"All these bugs sound yucky to me," said Max.

"You're not a hedgehog," replied Joe.
"They'll love it. But we'll also need to get some special meaty hedgehog or cat food. Some hedgehogs might be skinny due to illness when they come here and won't be able to eat bugs straight away."

WELCOME!

BUG BAR

CATERPILLAR CAFE

"Cheeky Tess
and Daisy Dot
are wondering
what's going on,"
said Mum.

"Welcome to Pricklington Palace!"

PRICKLY POND

HEDGEHOG HOME

"That's a great name," said Mum, laughing. "I've got some good news boys... Zoe the vet has volunteered to help us when we get very sick hedgehogs. I'm going to do some training too as we need to make sure we're doing things correctly."

"Thank you everyone for coming to the official opening of our hedgehog sanctuary," said Max, as mum handed out hedgehog-shaped cupcakes.

"Hedgehogs are officially classed as vulnerable to extinction and we are losing them at the same rate as we are losing tigers," said Joe, reading from his notes. "We want to do our best to help as may as we can and we hope you'll join us."

"I'd like to introduce you to Lady Scabbers, our very first resident. Zoe the vet just brought her over," said Mum.

"But... she's so ugly, she doesn't even look like a REAL hedgehog. She's got so many scabs," whispered Max.

"She is unique; beautiful in her own way.
Do you see the scars on her back? They were
caused by someone cutting their grass with a
strimmer and now she can't curl up. She was
found wandering around in the daytime and
that's always a warning sign as hedgehogs
should only come out at night," said Mum.

"We've got to give her a medicated bath,"
said Mum.
"I'll get the towel," replied Max.

"And I'll get the special oil so she can have a massage. That'll help her skin," said Joe.

"Once we've done that, I'll give her an injection and she can have her dinner. Then it'll be time for her to have a nap on the heat pad," added Mum.

"I can't believe the difference in Lady Scabbers," said Zoe. " To see her playing by the pond and exploring the bug hotel is incredible."

"We can't believe it either," said Mum. "She's still very wobbly but she's such a happy hedgehog. Joe and Max have done an amazing job."

"They sure have, they've saved her life!
I'd like to bring over any other sick hedgehogs
I get, if that's okay?"

"Hey Daisy Dot, you cheeky goat, that food was meant for the hedgehogs," said Joe.

"We've got TEN hungry hedgehogs to feed tonight and TWO more coming tomorrow," agreed Max.

"I love being a hedgehog rescuer," said Max.

"I do too," said Joe. "Helping animals is the best thing ever!"

eeek!

eeek!

"Can you hear that noise?" said Mum. "It sounds like a baby bird..."

"It's hoglets in the log pile!"
said Joe, racing over.

"Our first baby hedgehogs,"
said Max. "How exciting!"

www.ingramcontent.com/pod-product-compliance
Lightning Source LLC
LaVergne TN
LVHW072115070426
835510LV00002B/68

* 9 7 8 0 7 2 2 3 5 4 2 1 6 *